Dream Big!
Carol L Schulz
♡

The Story Of Journey
The Great Horned Owl

Written and Illustrated by Carol L Schultz
Journey's Story by Phyllis Carlson

This Book Belongs To

Jefferson, Alex and Ben Redjohns

from

Grandpa and Grandma Carlson

2024

The Story Of Journey
The Great Horned Owl

Written and Illustrated by Carol L Schultz
Journey's Story by Phyllis Carlson

Copyright 2023 Schultz Publishing

Publishing Coordination, Stacey Willey
Globe Printing Inc.
Ishpeming, Michigan

ISBN 979-8-9870288-1-0

No portion of this publication may be reproduced, reprinted or otherwise copied for distribution purposes without express written permission by the author.

This book is dedicated to all Wildlife Rehabilitaters who care for injured or orphaned wildlife.

And to "Journey" a Great Horned Owl, who has dedicated his life to teach humans about his species.

Thank you to my family and friends for all the love and encouragement they have shown me over the years.

A special Thank You to Phyllis Carlson for sharing her story about "Journey" the Great Horned Owl.

FORWARD

The story of "Journey, the Great Horned Owl" is the truelife story of a young injured owl named Journey who is cared for by a Wildlife Rehabilitator named Phyllis Carlson from Quinnesec, Michigan.

I first approached Phyllis in December of 2022 when I read an article in the The Daily News about Journey, the Great Horned Owl and his caregiver Phyllis.

I thought the story about Journey would make a great story to tell children and adults alike about the life of Journey, the Great Horned Owl.

The young owl was struck by a car when he was out learning to hunt for food. Because his wing was badly injured, Journey would never be able to fly again. He would need special care to survive from someone who had the knowledge to care for a wild animal.

Phyllis Carlson was that person. As a Wildlife Rehabilitator who has cared for multiple wild animals over the years, Phyllis was ready to take on the challenge and commitment for his care. She decided to expand her role of rehabber and become an educator. She applied for the necessary permits to make Journey an educational Owl.

Over the years Journey and Phyllis have done multiple programs to young and old alike about the Magnificent Great Horned Owl.

I hope you enjoy the story of Journey. Included along with the story are additional "Owl Facts" to learn about the Great Horned Owl.

The Story of Journey

The Great Horned Owl

  Journey's story begins during the cold snowy winter of 2000 - 2001.

  Journey was born in an old pine tree in the Quinnesec Cemetery of Dickinson County, Michigan.

  Some of the pine trees in the cemetery were 100 years old. It was a perfect place for a Great Horned Owl to be born.

Journey was one of two eggs that were laid by the Mother Great Horned Owl. The Great Horned Owl starts nesting in the winter.

The incubation period (the process in which an egg develops until the young chick is ready to hatch) is usually from 30 - 37 days.

The adult Owls do not build the nest, but use a nest that another bird has used, or will use a hollow tree or old building.

The Mother Owl rarely moves from the nest, protecting the eggs from the snow and cold.

The Father Owl captures food and brings it to the Mother Owl while she keeps the eggs warm and safe.

By the end of March to early April, the eggs have hatched. The owlets are covered in fine, soft feathers called "down."

The "down" is grayish white, gradually soft downy feathers come in that are a light brown.

The Mother Owl still continues to keep them warm and protected and the Father continues to hunt for food for the Mother and babies.

In late spring the little owls feathers are starting to come in.

They can't fly yet, but they leave the nest and move around the branches of the tree that their nest is in.

They are now called "branchers."

By early June, the feathers of the young owls have grown in enough that they are able to start flying.

They talk to each other and their parents by calling in high pitched screeches.

At first the young owls are not very good hunters, but the parents continue to feed them during the summer.

Sometimes a strong wind blowing can cause them to tumble to the ground, but the young owls climb back up the tree using their beak and sharp talons.

By July the young owls are 4 months old and are able to fly.

One day Journey hears a mouse rustling in the leaves across the road. He flew towards the rustling and did not notice the car approaching and the people in the car did not see Journey.

As Journey flies across the road, he is hit by the car. Journey lands next to a fence on the side of the road. He tries to fly, but his wing is badly injured.

Journey notices a man walking towards him. The man's name is Steve. Journey tries to hide in the leaves, but Steve stops and looks at Journey and notices that he is hurt.

Steve knows there is a Wildlife Rehabilitator named Phyllis who can help Journey.

When Steve tells Phyllis about the injured owl, Phyllis and her husband Walt go to try and help the owl.

They find Journey next to the fence, he is very frightened (he doesn't know Phyllis wants to help him). He starts to click his beak and hiss at her.

Phyllis cautiously approaches the frightened little owl. Phyllis has a special permit and has cared for wild animals for many years. She knows how to handle Journey very carefully.

Phyllis has a special pair of thick leather gloves to protect her hands and arms from Journey's sharp talons.

Because of Wildlife Rehabilitators like her, injured wild animals can be cared for and (most of them) can be returned to the wild.

Phyllis took him to a Veterinarian (A Doctor who cares for sick and injured animals).

The Veterinarian told Phyllis that Journey's wing was badly broken. He would not be able to fly anymore.

Phyllis was sad for Journey, but she had an idea, she could get the permits needed and Journey could become an educational Ambassador for owls.

In 2003 Phyllis and Journey began to do programs together to teach people about the magnificent Owl. Phyllis named him Journey because it became his life journey to teach humans about his species.

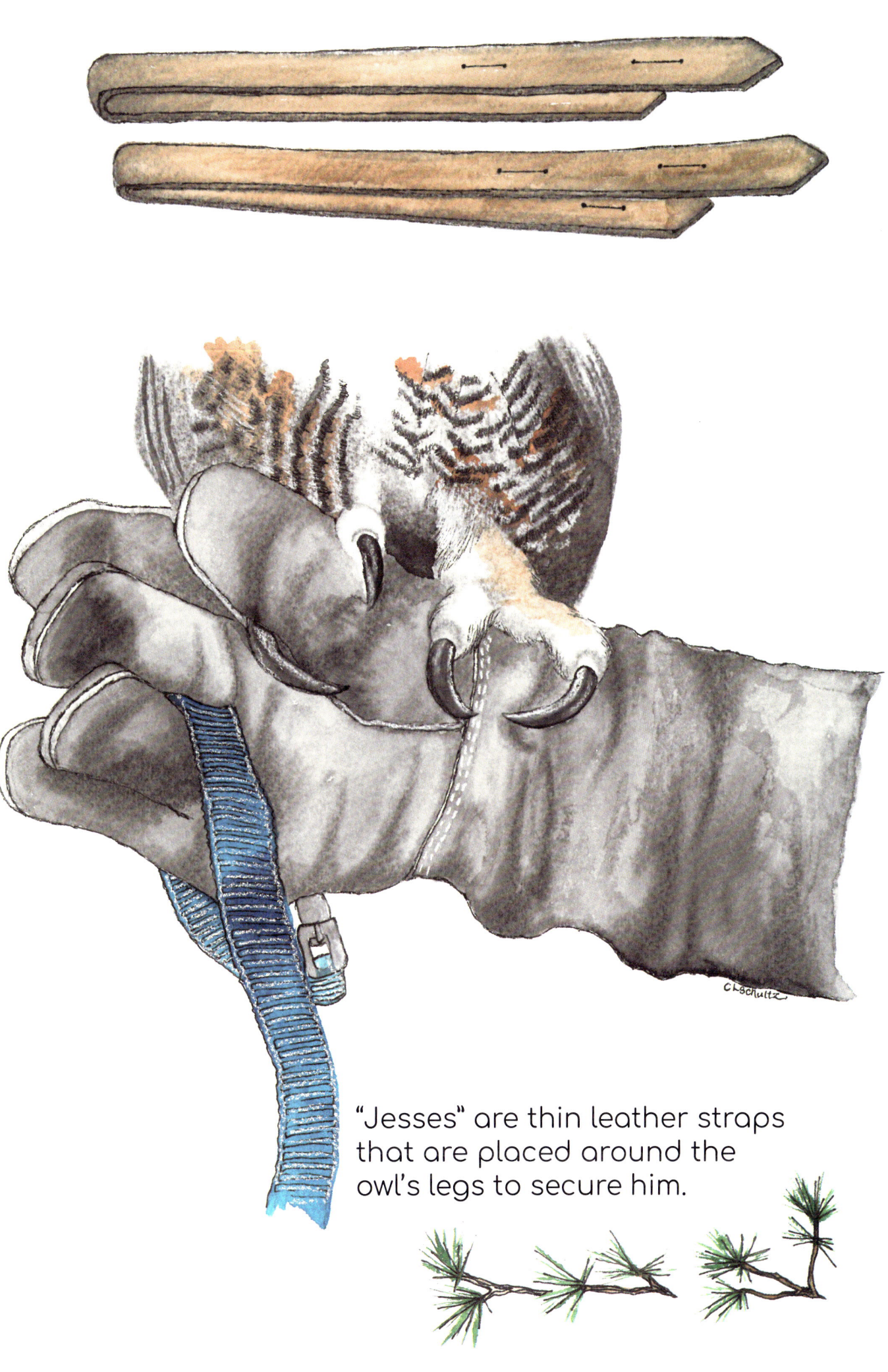

"Jesses" are thin leather straps that are placed around the owl's legs to secure him.

More Facts About the GREAT HORNED OWL

Owls are wild animals and it is illegal to keep them as a pet. Wildlife Rehabilitators are required to have permits to care for wild animals.

The Great Horned Owl has a barrel shaped body. They weigh between 3 and 6 pounds. Their call is "HOOT, HOOT, HOOT"

 EYES

The owls eyes are large.
The pupil's open to let the light in and close to keep the light out. The iris is yellow.

They only see in black, white and gray.
In the back of their eyes they have light sensitive receptors called "Rods." Owls can see 100 times better in dim light than we can.

The owl can't turn its eyes, but must turn its whole head to look around. However it's an old wives tale that an owl can turn its head in circles, It can only turn its head about 270 degrees.

EARS and EAR TUFTS

The ears on a Great Horned Owl are not on top of their head, but are small slits located on the side of their head at the edge of the facial disc.

The ears are asymmetrical (not the same height) on the sides of the owl's head.
Ear "Tufts" are not ears, they are just feathers.

Only ¼ of owl species have ear tufts.
The ear "Tufts" on the owlet's head are covered with fine feathers and look like little puffs.

The adult ear "Tufts" are larger and covered with feathers, and are used for camouflage.

The tufts help to break up the shape of the owl and make it look like part of the branches around it.

The "facial discs" surround the eyes and help to funnel sound to the owl's ears.

An owl can hear a mouse ½ mile away and beneath the snow.
(Now THAT'S good hearing!)

WINGS

Their wings are large and broad compared to their body size.

The leading edge of the feather has "serrations" (comb-like hooks on the outer edge of the feather.)

Because of the "serrations" the Great Horned Owl is capable of "silent flight," they are able to fly without making any noise.

The structure (parts) of the wing also allows the owl to fly at a very low speed.

FEET and TALONS

Owls' feet are feathered to help insulate them against the cold.

They are powerful hunters that grip their prey with their extremely sharp talons.

FOOD and PELLETS

Most of the food the owl eats are small rodents. They also eat rabbits, small mammals and other birds.

They will eat skunks (and not many animals eat skunks), good thing the owl does not have a good sense of smell!

The owl cannot digest the fur and bones of the animals it eats. They "regurgitate" (throw up) a "pellet" that is made up of the fur and bones.

Sometimes you can find these "pellets" on the ground at the base of a tree that an owl has been sitting in.

ABOUT THE WILDLIFE REHABILITATOR

I grew up in Northern VA. There were woods surrounding our neighborhood and I would spend all day wandering them.

My parents fostered my love of animals of all kinds including turtles, snakes and other wildlife.

I moved to the Upper Peninsula in the early 70's and ended up in the Iron Mountain area in 1975. At that time Fred Kangas of Kingsford, known as the" Bird Man," cared for orphaned and injured birds.

Occasionally someone would bring me an animal that needed help. I particularly remember a Robin with a broken leg that I splinted, it healed and I released it back into the wild.

After Mr. Kangas passed away, I ended up with a few more animals, but was not officially rehabbing. It wasn't until the late 1980's when I moved to Quinnesec, Michigan that I started caring for wildlife on a more regular basis. One of my neighbors was a DNR biologist, who would bring me animals to care for.

By the mid 1990's I had received my state permit and was an official Wildlife Rehabilitator. I joined the National Wildlife Rehabilitators Association. I would go to conferences where I would take classes on wound management and species specific care. I got my first Federal permit for birds and became the only person in the Upper Peninsula that was permitted for birds. Between birds and small mammals I was quite busy, while also working full time as a 911 Dispatcher for Dickinson County.

I was grateful when several years later another woman moved to Kingsford and had permits to care for small birds.

Eventually, bird rehab centers opened in Gladstone, Michigan and Marquette, Michigan and my workload became more manageable.

After over 30 years of rehabbing, I retired at the end of 2021.

I also decided to "retire" Journey from doing programs at the end of 2022. At almost 22 years old, (mid 80's in human years) Journey has begun to show his age.

ABOUT THE AUTHOR/ ILLUSTRATOR

"Journey, the Great Horned Owl" brought back special memories of spending time on the family farm in Sagola, Michigan when I was young. I would stay at the farm for one week during the summer and hang out with my cousins.

I can still picture the full moon at night through the bedroom window and hear the 'HOOT, HOOT, HOOT" of the Owl (and the lonely sound of the train whistle).

With the windows open at night to let in the cool breeze after the heat of the day, the sound of the Owl was comforting to me.

When I started this book, it was easy for me to picture the illustrations and "hear" the story of "Journey" in my imagination.

I have been drawing and painting for as long as I can remember. When I described how good I feel when I am creating art, a relative told me that it was "mental yoga."

I hope you enjoy the true story of "Journey, The Great Horned Owl."

Carol L Schultz

To order additional books
"Journey, The Great Horned Owl"
or "The Adventures of Charlie the Chihuahua"
email Carol Schultz: rockywaterart@gmail.com
or clschultz5.cs@gmail.com